Greater Than a Tourist
Ann Arbor
Michigan
USA

50 Travel Tips from a Local

Kaisa Wayrynen

Copyright © 2017 CZYK Publishing
All Rights Reserved. No part of this publication may be reproduced, including scanning and photocopying, or distributed in any form or by any means, electronic or mechanical, or stored in a database or retrieval system without prior written permission from the publisher.

Disclaimer: The publisher has put forth an effort in preparing and arranging this book. The information provided herein by the author is provided "as is". Use this information at your own risk. Consult your doctor before engaging in any medical activities. The publisher and author disclaim any liabilities for any loss of profit or commercial or personal damages resulting from the information contained in this book.

Order Information: To order this title please email lbrenenc@gmail.com or visit GreaterThanATourist.com. A bulk discount can be provided.

Cover Template Creator: Lisa Rusczyk Ed. D. using Canva.
Cover Creator: Lisa Rusczyk Ed. D.
Image: By Dwight Burdette (Own work) [CC BY 3.0 (http://creativecommons.org/licenses/by/3.0)], via Wikimedia Commons

CZYK
PUBLISHING

Lock Haven, PA
All rights reserved.
ISBN: 9781549793370

>TOURIST

Kaisa Wayryn

BOOK DESCRIPTION

Are you excited about planning your next trip?

Do you want to try something new?

Would you like some guidance from a local?

If you answered yes to any of these questions, then this Greater Than a Tourist book is for you.

Greater Than a Tourist—Ann Arbor, MI by Kaisa Wayrynen offers the inside scoop on Ann Arbor, Michigan. Most travel books tell you how to sightsee. Although there's nothing wrong with that, as a part of the Greater than a Tourist series, this book will give you tips from someone who lives at your next travel destination. In these pages, you'll discover local advice that will help you throughout your trip.

Travel like a local. Slow down and get to know the people and the culture of a place. By the time you finish this book, you will be eager and prepared to travel to your next destination.

Kaisa Wayryn

TABLE OF CONTENTS

BOOK DESCRIPTION

TABLE OF CONTENTS

DEDICATION

ABOUT THE AUTHOR

HOW TO USE THIS BOOK

FROM THE PUBLISHER

WELCOME TO > TOURIST

INTRODUCTION

1. Attend the Summer Festival

2. Watch a College Football Game

3. Get a Sandwich at Zingerman's

4. Get Artsy at the Art Fair

5. Take a Stroll through the Arboretum

6. Get a Drink at Ashley's

7. Toss a Frisbee in the Diag

8. Visit the Gum Wall

9. Find a Fairy Door

10. See a Film at the Michigan Theater

11. Eat Local at the Farmer's Market

12. Paddle on the Huron River

13. Go on a Craft Brewery Tour

14. Touch Cool Stuff at the Hands-On Museum

15. Visit the Botanical Gardens

16. Meditate in the Law Quad

17. Picnic in Gallup Park

18. Explore Kerrytown

19. Learn at the Natural History Museum

20. Experience Nature at the Leslie Science Center

21. Walk Down Main Street

22. Pet Farm Animals at Domino's Farms

23. Hike at Bird Hills

24. Shop at the Robot Shop

25. Get Bubble Tea

26. Support the University Musical Society

27. Sit Back and Enjoy the Water Hill Music Festival

28. Grab a Cup of Local Joe

29. Visit the UMMA

30. See a Performance at Hill Auditorium

31. Check Out a Presidential Library

32. Walk Down State Street

33. Watch Performing Arts at the Power Center

34. Eat Ice Cream at Washtenaw Dairy

35. See the Christmas Lights

36. Listen to Live Music at the Blind Pig

37. Get Rustic at Cobblestone Farm

38. Spend Your Quarters at Pinball Pete's

39. Eat Healthy at Sava's

40. Gift Shop Downtown

41. Drink Tea at Crazy Wisdom

42. Treat Yourself to Dinner at the Gandy Dancer

43. Eat Breakfast for Dinner at Fleetwood

44. Take a Day Trip to Greenfield Village

45. Visit the Kelsey Museum of Archaeology

46. Watch the Puck Drop on NYE

47. Eat Palestinian Food at Jerusalem Garden

48. Stroll Through Nickels Arcade

Kaisa Wayryn

49. Catch a Show at The Ark

50. Go Ice Skating at Yost

Top Reasons to Book This Trip

Our Story

Notes

DEDICATION

This book is dedicated to free spirits, intellectuals, and oddballs of Ann Arbor, MI, who shaped me into the happy hippie vagabond I am. The welcoming culture of positivity in Ann Arbor is a rare and beautiful thing. I feel lucky to have grown up in such an open-minded place, as it has taught me to open my mind to every place I have been since. Those good Ann Arbor vibes will always be there for anyone who is lucky enough to travel to this wonderful town.

Kaisa Wayryn

ABOUT THE AUTHOR

Kaisa Wayrynen is a travel writer who currently lives in Watford City, North Dakota, where she is working as a National Park Service Ranger.

Kaisa loves to travel and be one with nature. She grew up in Ann Arbor, Michigan, a town known for its parks, rivers, and abundance of trees. She learned to love the outdoors from a young age, and since graduating from Wellesley College she has traveled the world volunteering on organic farms and working in National Parks.

Kaisa Wayryn

HOW TO USE THIS BOOK

The Greater Than a Tourist book series was written by someone who has lived in an area for over three months. The goal of this book is to help travelers either dream or experience different locations by providing opinions from a local. The author has made suggestions based on their own experiences. Please do your own research before traveling to the area in case the suggested places are unavailable.

Kaisa Wayryn

FROM THE PUBLISHER

Traveling can be one of the most important parts of a person's life. The anticipation and memories that you have are some of the best. As a publisher of the Greater Than a Tourist book series, as well as the popular 50 Things to Know book series, we strive to help you learn about new places, spark your imagination, and inspire you. Wherever you are and whatever you do I wish you safe, fun, and inspiring travel.

Lisa Rusczyk Ed. D.

CZYK Publishing

Kaisa Wayryn

WELCOME TO > TOURIST

Kaisa Wayryn

INTRODUCTION

I love to travel the world. I'll admit, nothing gets me quite as excited as whipping out my passport for an international flight. Everyone has a home base, however, in one way or another. My home is Ann Arbor, Michigan, and I am grateful for that every single day, wherever I am. Ann Arbor is special; those who grew up there know it, and those who travel there see it.

Ann Arbor is a college football-loving town with truly something for everyone. Whether you are an art lover, a nature lover, or just a plain ol' foodie, you will find your joy in Ann Arbor. That's because Ann Arbor is one of the most positive, openminded towns in America. It certainly has the highest concentration of hippies in the Midwest, anyway. The town is home to a number of annual music and arts festivals, but boasts a wonderful Farmer's Market and local shopping year round.

Kaisa Wayryn

1. Attend the Summer Festival

The annual Ann Arbor Summer Festival, known to locals as Top of the Park or "Top", is a month-long celebration of local food and music. It's a huge staple in the Ann Arbor community; every Ann Arbor kid's favorite time of year was Top of the Park season. Spend the evening sampling from local food stalls (or for the 21+ crowd, beer tent), listening to up-and-coming Midwestern bands, and catching whatever movie is projected on the big screen at the end of the night. It happens in June or July, so Michigan evenings will vary from cool and breezy to sweltering hot. Either way, bring some friends and a blanket to lie on and enjoy an iconic Ann Arbor summer eve.

2. Watch a College Football Game

Go Blue! If you want to live like a true Ann Arborite, you need to spend a chilly fall morning cheering on the Michigan Wolverines at the Big House. I didn't even attend the University of Michigan, but after growing up in here I am a Michigan Wolverine in my heart and soul. At its heart, Ann Arbor is a college town. College football is deeply ingrained in the culture here, and you'll see plenty of maize and blue to prove it.

The atmosphere at the Big House on its own is something very special to behold, particularly when we're playing Ohio State or Michigan State!

3. Get a Sandwich at Zingerman's

Any local will tell you that if you can only eat one meal in Ann Arbor, it should be at Zingerman's Delicatessen. Not just that—you should eat a sandwich at Zingerman's. It's almost a rite of passage. Though each local's individual recommendation varies, if you're a fan of corned beef and pastrami the Jon & Amy's Double Dip can't be beat. It was named after my parents' friends who met working at Zingerman's as youngsters.

Zingerman's opened in 1982 and has been Ann Arbor's hot spot for brisket, bagels, brownies and, yes, sandwiches, ever since! Now you can buy locally made artisanal bread, pastry, cream cheese, and candy bars in their attached shop. If you understandably get addicted to Zingerman's while in Ann Arbor, you can even order online from their website!

4. Get Artsy at the Art Fair

The Ann Arbor Art Fair has gotta be tied with the Summer Festival as the main events in an Ann Arbor summer. Local stores host huge Art Fair sales as downtown streets shut down to car traffic and artists' booths pop up everywhere.

From ceramics to photography, watercolors to oil paintings, the Art Fair seriously has it all. Get there earlier in the day to avoid crowds, though, since it seems to be getting bigger and more popular every year.

5. Take a Stroll through the Arboretum

Nichols Arboretum, affectionately referred to by locals as "the Arb", is basically Ann Arbor's Central Park, only much more peaceful. If you're going to visit one park or nature area, this is probably the most classic Ann Arbor choice. Open sunrise to sunset just East of downtown, it's actually walking distance from many Ann Arbor highlights. There's tons of parking in the area, too, though.

Once you get there you can go for a stroll through grassy fields and forested areas and play some pickup soccer. You see a wide variety of folks hanging in the Arb, from college students to families to runners. It's big enough that you could easily get lost for a bit, but that's part of the fun!

The mosquitos can be brutal in the evening, so bring your bug spray if the season requires it!

6. Get a Drink at Ashley's

Ashley's Craft Beer and Gastropub on State Street is one of Ann Arbor's most iconic places to go for a cold one. It has been a favorite of University of Michigan students for literal generations (1983, specifically). It has an energetic, social atmosphere in the summer and a warm, almost cozy feel in the winter. It has a huge selection of local beer and imported beer alike! Indeed, the beer selection is definitely Ashley's claim to fame.

Besides just the beer, though, Ashley's serves a mean burger and fries. The service is amazing and I've never known anyone to have a bad experience there. If you want to truly eat (and drink!) like a local, whether college student, professor, or townie, you gotta stop by.

7. Toss a Frisbee in the Diag

I can't tell you how many awesome memories I've made in the Diag. I think many locals feel the same way. Grab a coffee or a bubble tea from nearby South University, find a bench in the shade (or a nice patch of grass!), and let the Ann Arbor vibes soak in. The Diag is located smack dab in the middle of University of Michigan's campus. During the academic year the Diag is full of students going to and from classes or just chilling out. It's surrounded by University buildings, but the path through it is like a scenic bridge linking the South University area and the rest of downtown.

Ann Arbor is a super safe city, so walking through the Diag after dark is a favorite pastime. Many romantic date nights have found their way here. It's also just a great place to stop and take a breather in between shopping and exploring Ann Arbor.

8. Visit the Gum Wall

It's exactly what it sounds like. Stay with me.

The gum wall is an art display by the people, for the people. It is located in Graffiti Alley, on the corner of Liberty and Maynard (yes, "Graffiti Alley" comes up on Google Maps). Over the years, people have all stuck their gum on the same wall and now it's been spray painted to look artsy and awesome like the rest of Graffiti Alley. It's millions of pieces of gum on a wall that has been turned into art. What more could you want?! Even if that big wall of old germs doesn't appeal to you, Graffiti Alley itself is an urban art experience you can't miss. Locals will have mad respect for you if you make it a priority on your Ann Arbor trip.

9. Find a Fairy Door

As if a wall of gum wasn't enough, Ann Arbor is also famous for its collection of tiny, colorful fairy doors dotting the city. I told you this place was quirky. I'm not even positive how many there are, though the official Fairy Doors of Ann Arbor Wikipedia page will tell you there are seven! They're all differently decorated and about the size of a boot.

If you want to make it a scavenger hunt to find all of them, it would be a unique way to explore Ann Arbor and chat with local business owners. Best of all, this activity is completely free!

I'll even give you a head start: one door is inside of Sweetwaters Cafe on West Washington, and another is just outside the Peaceable Kingdom store on South Main. I included these two doors because Sweetwaters has amazing Italian sodas and Peaceable Kingdom is my favorite gift shop in Ann Arbor.

10. See a Film at the Michigan Theater

The gigantic lit-up sign for the Michigan Theater is seriously one of the most famous Ann Arbor images I can think of. They don't show the current Hollywood hits so much as smaller indie flicks or "fine films". I think the first movie I ever saw there was called Winged Migration, and the most recent was Black Swan. I swear they don't only show movies about birds.

You buy your ticket in an old-fashioned ticket window and enter to the grand foyer. It's one of the most gorgeous rooms in the city. The theaters themselves are just as beautifully decorated. I'm pretty sure they have actual floor-length velvet curtains on either side of the screen, though that may have changed by now.

The theater opened in 1928, but was established as it's current not-for-profit model in 1979. It is ran totally by community volunteers who know and love it.

"Why do you go away? So that you can come back. So that you can see the place you came from with new eyes and extra colors. And the people there see you differently, too. Coming back to where you started is not the same as never leaving."

—Terry Pratchett

Kaisa Wayryn

11. Eat Local at the Farmer's Market

I'm obviously biased, but the Ann Arbor Farmer's Market is the best in the world. It's open year-round every Saturday, and also on Wednesdays from May to December. Obviously, the fresh produce selections vary depending on when you're there.

With Ann Arbor's outdoorsy, hippie-ish attitudes, it's no wonder it has a well-established and extremely popular Farmer's Market. I have to admit, the only time I've felt super crowded in Ann Arbor besides Art Fair and Summer Festival has been at the weekly Farmer's Market.

Head to Kerrytown early if you want to avoid bigger crowds. The market opens at 7 AM during the summer, 8 AM during the winter. There's something for everyone, that's for sure. You've got the basics, like Michigan-grown fruit, veggies, and nuts, but also more eccentric options like yogurt, saurkraut, and even homemade sriracha.

12. Paddle on the Huron River

As if the plethora of parks and green spaces wasn't appealing enough to the outdoorsman or woman, Ann Arbor is right on the Huron River. That means every summer we canoe or kayak at least once.

Skip's Canoe Livery on East Delhi Road is the place my friends and I prefer. They offer a bus service so you can actually canoe or kayak miles down the river and get back to your vehicle. Those other destinations are Husdon Mills Metropark and Dexter-Huron Metropark. The prices and schedules change kind of often, so I'd call first to make sure they'll have something that works for you.

13. Go on a Craft Brewery Tour

Like any college town worth it's salt, Ann Arbor has an impressive craft beer scene. Michigan in general is coming onto that scene in a big way lately, with Ann Arbor an epicenter of it.

The best part? Downtown Ann Arbor is small enough that you can hit several excellent breweries within walking distance. My personal favorites are Arbor Brewing Company, Homes Brewery, and Wolverine State Brewing Company. If that's not enough, I'd add Jolly Pumpkin, Grizzly Peak, and Blue Tractor to your brewery to-do list (or should I say, to-brew list!). One of the many wonderful things about craft breweries is the attention to detail that starts with their beer and extends to their food. All of these places are delicious lunch or dinner stops as well.

14. Touch Cool Stuff at the Hands-On Museum

I don't care how old you are, the Ann Arbor Hands-On Museum is a gosh dang good time. It is located on Ann Street and as of 2017 charged $12 per person (toddlers 2 and under are free). There are sometimes special exhibits or activities, such as live animal educational demonstrations. Certain days of the year are solely dedicated to activities for kids with sensory sensitivities and difficulties.

There's a preschool gallery for the super young ones, but tons of exhibits for all ages, too. My favorite was always the Michigan Nature exhibit. Be careful: if you take your kid in here, they may never want to leave!

15. Visit the Botanical Gardens

I tried to make this list as walkable as possible, but this one does require a vehicle. Don't worry, it's worth the drive.
About 15 minutes outside of downtown Ann Arbor, the Matthaei Botanical Gardens on Dixboro Road are truly an unmissable highlight. If you are at all into greenhouses or nature walks, they will not disappoint.
The two main parts of the Botanical Gardens are just that: a series of greenhouses, and a huge expanse of outdoor garden and forest to explore. The greenhouses are organized by environment and have such an impressive collection of plant species. The outdoor gardens are of course most spectacular in the spring and summer, but there's something silent and peaceful about walking through them in the snowy winter. Past the gardens, you can walk through some woods, dotted with gazebos and all the babbling brooks you could want. This area is also great for bird watching!

16. Meditate in the Law Quad

The University of Michigan William W. Cook Law Quadrangle is like the Diag's quieter, more elegant older sister. The first time I walked through it in high school, I felt like I'd been transported to a grassy European courtyard. It's a lovely, shaded green surrounded by gorgeous buildings and perfect for a romantic picnic or just sitting and reading a book.

The Gothic buildings surrounding the Quad include residences for law students, classrooms, and the Allan F. and Alene Smith Library. Even if you're not into lawyer stuff, check it out; it's apparently one of the best law libraries in the world.

17. Picnic in Gallup Park

Fun fact! Gallup Park, Ann Arbor's most visited recreation area on the Huron River, is right across from my high school. Huron High School, to be exact, on Fuller Road. This area is about 15 minutes East of downtown Ann Arbor by car. Gallup Park is another option for canoe rentals for checking out the Huron River up close and personal.

There's much more to do than canoe on Gallup's 69 green acres. There are tons of scenic paths and bridges to the small islands along the river. There are two playgrounds, plus picnic shelters and grills for a real picnic for the whole family.

18. Explore Kerrytown

Kerrytown is a Historic Market District neighborhood known for cool shops, great food, and red brick buildings. It's just barely North of the heart of downtown Ann Arbor. Parking is a huge pain, though, so if testing your parallel parking skills sounds unappealing I'd park in a lot downtown and walk to Kerrytown. The most popular Kerrytown restaurant is probably Zingerman's, but the Farmer's Market is location here, as well. The little shops are fun and quirky; Kerrytown has a spice store, a tea store, and a stationary/paper store.

There are special holiday events, so check their website to see what's on the schedule.

19. Learn at the Natural History Museum

The University of Michigan Museum of Natural History is a short walk from the Diag/downtown Ann Arbor, just East of town. It's incredibly impressive and extensive for a Natural History Museum outside of a major city. It's not AMNH or the Field Museum, but it's closer than you'd think. The exhibit halls are beautifully organized, taking you on a journey through time and evolution. Of course, the fossil hall is quite the crowd pleaser. The museum has a huge mammoth mounted in the center of the hall, with an equally impressive display of prehistoric whales. These themes are directly influenced by the focuses of the University of Michigan paleontology department's research, which has been groundbreaking. Yes, there are dinosaurs, too.

20. Experience Nature at the Leslie Science Center

If you're starting to notice a theme, namely that many Ann Arbor activities have an outdoorsy/nature focus to them, you're absolutely right. The Leslie Science and Nature Center is no exception.

While there are plenty of experiences to be had at the Leslia Science center, three main things to experience here are the science center's raptor enclosure, critter house, and black pond wood. The raptor enclosure is an outdoor exhibit dedicated to educating the public on birds of prey, open all year except the dead of winter when it's too chilly for them. You can see educational talks and even feedings! The critter house is a small menagerie of mostly reptiles and amphibians, which sometimes get taken out of their cages for educational programs. Black pond wood is an exciting boardwalk hike through a typical Michigan forest wetland!

"Wherever you go becomes a part of you somehow."

—Anita Desai

Kaisa Wayryn

21. Walk Down Main Street

This one is short, simple, and a great way to see the "real" Ann Arbor. Just talk a walk down Main Street! Ann Arbor's Main Street is true to its name in that many of the city's most popular businesses are located here.

Honestly, I've lived in this city most of my life and I still get a kick out of taking a walk down Main. During the day there's a lot going on, of course, but even a nighttime walk can feel like you're experiencing the city lights of a much bigger city with the action all around you.

22. Pet Farm Animals at Domino's Farms

This one is a bit out of downtown, and by that I mean a 20 minute drive Northeast (that's another thing you'll notice about Michiganders, we always measure distance in drive time). But I mean, it's a petting farm. I'd drive through the night in a blizzard for fluffy lamb cuddles.

I was amazed to see that, as of 2017, admission is still only $6 per person, considering the size of the grounds and diversity of farm animals they maintain there. It was established in 1984 by the founder of Domino's pizza, though tragically there was no pizza for sale there last time I checked.

It's really just good old fashioned farm-themed fun, a tribute to the farmers who used to live in the area.

23. Hike at Bird Hills

If you assumed a town called Ann Arbor would be full of trees, congrats, you are correct! Trees, parks, and nature areas abound. I have it on good authority that the favorite Ann Arbor hiking spot of park rangers is Bird Hills Nature Area. As of 2017 there weren't facilities, so use the bathroom, fill water bottles, and pack a lunch before you go.

The miles of unpaved trail are my absolutely favorite for trail runs. They really give you an idea of why Ann Arbor is so full of nature lovers. The beech and dogwood trees are my personal favorite, though there are plenty of other trees and wildflowers to make any botanist happy! The diversity and abundance of plant species actually wasn't an accident; they were planted purposefully to make the land more appealing to developers, once upon a time. Thankfully, Bird Hills just remains an awesome place to hike today.

24. Shop at the Robot Shop

On Liberty and Main you will find a most curious Ann Arbor shopping destination. That is, of course, the Liberty Street Robot Supply and Repair.

This adorable little robot themed gift shop is actually the store associated with 826 Michigan, a nonprofit writing center. The writing center is also located here. Besides quirky robot kits and models, the store sells student's publications. There's also apparel and posters, the proceeds from all of which going to 826 Michigan's writing workshops and tutoring center. Here you can buy a coffee mug covered in robots, while supporting the literacy of local youth.

25. Get Bubble Tea

College towns have some of the most diverse and quirky food selections. Enter: bubble tea in Ann Arbor, Michigan. Bubble tea is basically a Taiwanese milky or fruity tea drink that gets its name from the tapioca balls/bubbles/boba inside. You drink it through a super wide straw and then chew the boba as you drink.

A few different restaurants around South University and downtown sell bubble tea, but the place I went to every week in high school was Bubble Island. My drink of choice was taro milk tea with the classic black bubbles (served warm or cold), but the possibilities are endless. For a refreshing summertime drink, the calpico coolers with little sweet jelly strips instead of tapioca balls are amazing. Bubble Island has tons of fun board games you can bring to your table and play while you drink. They even have food, like curly fries, popcorn chicken, and Japanese mochi ice cream balls!

26. Support the University Musical Society

Ann Arbor is all about supporting local artists. Get into that spirit by checking out one of the many, many musical offerings of the University Musical Society. They've been on the Ann Arbor music scene since 1879! There's a pretty wide, constantly changing variety of musical groups, from opera to jazz groups. String quartets tend to be a big hit, too. Regardless of what your particular tastes lead you to, live local music in relatively intimate venues make for a truly unique evening. The venues and prices of each performance differ.

27. Sit Back and Enjoy the Water Hill Music Festival

I say sit back and enjoy, because that is exactly how residents of Ann Arbor like to experience the annual Water Hill Music Festival (often fondly shortened to "Fest"). Residents get to sit back and enjoy from the comfort of their porches, if they live in the Water Hill neighborhood. Either that, or the residents are part of the music themselves and play their instrument from their own yard. The short and sweet description on Water Hill Fest's website says it all: "On the first Sunday in May a neighborhood erupts in song". The Fest prides itself on being a low key, laid back affair about the community's shared love of music. As such, there aren't food or beverages available at this Music Fest, only a bunch of happy music-lovers.

28. Grab a Cup of Local Joe

If you're a coffee drinker, you're gonna dig this city. There are more than a few local roasting joints to refuel at during your Ann Arbor visit.

Café Verde in the Kerrytown Food Co-Op uses all organic free trade ingredients to create their sometimes zany coffee drinks. If you're all about small batches and grass roots community involvement, Mighty Good Coffee Roasting Company is affiliated with a bunch of local businesses and nonprofits. The Lab Café is a decidedly hipster option with unique creations and delicious syrups.

My favorite? Sweetwaters. They're known for a huge drink menu so you will find something you like there.

29. Visit the UMMA

The University of Michigan Museum of Art (UMMA), is one of the largest University art museums in the whole country, and it shows. If art is your thing, I think you could spend a whole day here. Art isn't even really my thing and I could spend a whole day here.

They recommend parking on the streets around the museum or in whichever nearby structure suits your fancy. Admission is free, though a $10 donation is always appreciated.

Kaisa Wayryn

30. See a Performance at Hill Auditorium

University of Michigan's School of Theatre and Dance Hill Auditorium has been a venue for all manner of huge public events. It opened in 1913 and is one of campus's most striking buildings with huge stone columns standing at the front entrance. The interior is, of course, designed with acoustics and the audience in mind. All of this makes it a memorable place to see a music or theatrical performance!

The auditorium seats 3,500 and I've seen it fill up so if you can book ahead, that's a smart move. To give you an idea of just what their line-up is like in an average month, you could buy tickets for anything from a lecture series, philharmonic orchestra, or symphony band.

"The real voyage of discovery consists not in seeking new landscapes, but in having new eyes."

—*Marcel Proust*

Kaisa Wayryn

31. Check Out a Presidential Library

The Gerald R. Ford Presidential Library is a more subdued activity for the history buff traveling to Ann Arbor. Ford, the 38th President of the United States of America, was a University of Michigan graduate. He donated congressional papers and presidential materials to the University fairly early in his political career, and just kept it up! Obviously it's pretty exciting for any University to have a Presidential Library on site, so complete your University of Michigan Ann Arbor experience with a stop at Ford's.

You may have noticed that this is a Presidential Library, and not Museum. That's because the Gerald R. Ford Presidential Museum is over in Grand Rapids. It's worth a trip as well, if Presidential Museums are your cup of tea.

32. Walk Down State Street

Already got your Main Street stroll covered? I got another one for you, just a few blocks East. While State Street technically stretches for miles beyond downtown Ann Arbor, the stretch that passes through downtown is North State and its proximity to campus gives it an even more college town feel. You're visiting a college town, after all.

If you start at State and Huron, for example, heading South takes you past a ton of the items on this Top 50 list! You could stop for lunch and a drink at Ashley's before reaching the University of Michigan Museum of Art, and finish the afternoon with a relaxing rest in the Law Quad! Of course, Ann Arbor is all about the free spirits, so this is just a suggestion and I encourage you to do whatever you darn well feel like, in whatever order makes you happy.

33. Watch Performing Arts at the Power Center

The University of Michigan's School of Music Power Center for the Performing Arts (I know, it's a mouthful, you can just call it the Power Center) is a really unique space. The University website calls it their "most technically sophisticated performance space", because it was designed with performing arts in mind in 1963. All Ann Arbor had for big theatrical productions was Hill Auditorium, which was better suited to musical performances. The Power Center fixed that problem, with a design inspired by ancient Greek theatres and no seat farther than 80 feet from stage!

Even outside of the main theatre, it's an architecturally fascinating building. Check out their website for tickets and showtimes, or go to the University of Michigan Union downtown.

34. Eat Ice Cream at Washtenaw Dairy

Ann Arbor has a lot of ice cream options. Most locals will tell you the "can't miss" place, though, is Washtenaw Dairy. It's named after the county Ann Arbor is in and has been a beloved institution of that county for over 75 years. I can't tell you how many Saturday morning soccer games ended with ice cream and donuts at Washtenaw dairy. According to their website, their donuts are the only zero trans fats homemade donuts on the whole county. Pro-tip: their moose tracks will blow your mind. There are so many options to choose from it's hard to go wrong. The dairy fridge they have in the corner is also full of local fresh and delicious products, particularly the chocolate milk.

35. See the Christmas Lights

Walking through Ann Arbor after dark is frankly a cool experience any time of year. It's a funky little city with a lot of funky lights. That being said, the hands-down best time of year to see those city lights at night is the holidays. The streets of downtown are completely decked out and it's straight up magical. This is a moment when I am eternally grateful for Michigan's winters; there's nothing like a light snowfall as you walk through holiday lights and white streets.

Obviously Michigan gets cold in the winter, so dress appropriately. We have kind of a wet cold in Ann Arbor, so waterproof boots or shoes and warm socks will make or break your day tromping through the wintery streets.

36. Listen to Live Music at the Blind Pig

The Bling Pig's website says the following regarding Ann Arbor culture: "Ann Arbor has always been a cultural oasis of sorts - a plateau that protrudes through the lackluster blandness of small-town midwestern life, that provides a unique stepping stone between the industrial sprawl of Detroit and the thriving bustle of Chicago."

The downtown live music venue credits part of this "cultural oasis" atmosphere to the flourishing music scene, which the Blind Pig itself has played a part in cultivating. Some legit legends have graced the stage here as music has evolved over the past 50 years, though lesser known local artists make up a lot of the performers, too.

37. Get Rustic at Cobblestone Farm

The Cobblestone Farmhouse was constructed in 1845 and remains in all its glory as a museum and symbol of Ann Arbor's old rural lifestyles. Though its grounds are not as large as they once were, there is a big pretty lawn and trees all around the idyllic little farm house.

The Parks and Recreation Service technically run the space, but the Cobblestone Farm Association runs the tours. It's that association you'll want to call to schedule or tour or ask about hours and events. Cobblestone farm is extremely popular for events and parties, and is often rented out.

38. Spend Your Quarters at Pinball Pete's

Pinball Pete's on South University is one of the most kid friendly activities in downtown Ann Arbor, though truly suitable for all ages. It's an old-school arcade that's survived the decades. The variety of pinball machines will actually make your head spin, as will the cacophony or arcade beeps and buzzes and flashing lights.

Games are cheap and plentiful, and it somehow never seems to be too crowded.

39. Eat Healthy at Sava's

Sava's is one of my top restaurant recommendations in Ann Arbor. It's been around over 20 years, growing steadily all the while, but still manages to stay very modern and relevant. It's simultaneously classic and cool. Sava's is also one of the only restaurants on this list I enthusiastically recommend for breakfast in particular! Their Mediterranean eggs and sweet potato latkes are some of my favorites. If you're into mimosas, Sava's won't disappoint, either. Their Sunday brunch buffet is out of this world.

Even better, Sava's uses only the best ingredients, often local.

40. Gift Shop Downtown

Besides the unique local shops I've listed here, Ann Arbor has a pretty much endless collection of one-of-a-kind stores. They range from incense-scented hippie shawl shops, to imported art from all corners of the globe, to colorful toy stores.

If a shop window looks interesting to you in downtown Ann Arbor, just go in, because I promise it'll be ten times more intriguing inside.

"Travel far enough, you meet yourself."

—David Mitchell

Kaisa Wayryn

41. Drink Tea at Crazy Wisdom

Crazy wisdom is a bookshop and tearoom by name, but so, so much more. Last time I was there, they decorated the entrance with Nepalese-esque prayer flags. The store is boasts what they refer to as "tea and wisdom" with a side of "material treasures and ethereal pleasures".

Their shop section has much more than books—you'll find art, healing crystals, jewelry, and more. If you get thirsty from perusing the eccentric shelves, head over to the tearoom for a cup of hot chai.

They also host events like poetry series and story nights!

42. Treat Yourself to Dinner at the Gandy Dancer

The Gandy Dancer is a luxurious fine dining experience that I heartily recommend, if your budget allows it. It's just so darn delicious, and this is from someone highly skeptical of so-called fancy food. Dinner for two, with drinks and tip, will easily run over $100. Their fresh seafood and location in the city's lavishly renovated historic train depot make for quite a glamorous evening. There is some controversy surrounding the Gandy Dancer, insofar as the conversion of the historic building into a fine dining establishment was seen as a sell-out move by some. However, the restaurant retains many elements of the old depot, both decorative and in its proximity to the tracks themselves. In other words, you won't forget you're in a train station.

43. Eat Breakfast for Dinner at Fleetwood

Blow your budget at the Gandy Dancer? Have no fear, there is a greasy spoon waiting for you at Fleetwood Diner.

When I was a child, a wise friend once told me: "Never go to Fleetwood Diner after midnight, Kaisa". Okay, so I've broken that rule a fair few times during my college years. I can assure you that despite Fleetwood's sketchy appearance, it's perfectly friendly as long as you don't pick any fights. In fact, some of my favorite Fleetwood trips have been in the wee hours after the bars close and nothing sounds better than hash browns and fried eggs.

Fleetwood is like a tiny tin box diner with barely enough tables, both inside and outside its walls of questionable stability. I've never eaten outside at Fleetwood, though I bet it would be fun for people watching. You never know who you'll see in this tiny diner, though, so sometimes the people watching is just as good inside!

44. Take a Day Trip to Greenfield Village

Okay, Greenfield Village isn't technically in Ann Arbor city limits. It's actually much closer to Detroit. Still, I would be remiss if I didn't recommend it to any traveler to Southeastern Michigan. When you enter Greenfield Village, you travel back in time. It's not truly a "village" in the sense that no one lives there and you can't drive your car through it, though you can take a ride in a classic antique car!

The Henry Ford Museum and much of Greenfield Village is an ode to Detroit's part in turn of the century auto industry. There are often historical reenactors to make the whole experience even more like you're traveling back in time.

45. Visit the Kelsey Museum of Archaeology

Yep, it's another University of Michigan Museum. This one is kind of just across from the Museum of Art, so it's really doable to combine the two into an afternoon of museum fun.

Besides the permanent classical, Mediterranean, and Egyptian artifact collections, the Kelsey Museum has rotating featured exhibits that are always very good. When I wrote this, they had a fascinating exhibit on cosmogonic tattoos I was dying to see. I'm sure by the time you visit it'll be some other equally awesome display.

Like the Museum of Art, admission is free but donations are highly encouraged.

46. Watch the Puck Drop on NYE

This tradition is almost so painfully Michigander-ish I laughed out loud when I typed it. It's exactly what it sounds like; at on New Year's Eve in downtown Ann Arbor, we drop a gigantic hockey puck instead of the typical midnight ball drop.

There are typically bands playing in the street, bars and restaurants are packed, and the energy is upbeat and excited for the New Year. I never knew being outside after midnight in January in Michigan could be so much fun, until I watched the puck dropped and joined in the surrounding festivities.

As an added bonus, Christmas lights are still up, so the streets are absolutely popping with light (and champagne)!

47. Eat Palestinian Food at Jerusalem Garden

Bet you didn't think you could get insanely delicious Palestinian food in the Northern Midwest. Literally anything you eat at Jerusalem Garden will be satisfying and pleasing to the palate. My favorite is just a good plain ole falafel with some Turkish coffee (and maybe some baklava for dessert).

This family-own restaurant is open Monday through Saturdays on Liberty Street. It has grown in popularity since opening in 1987, and for good reason. I have yet to eat better Middle Eastern food anywhere in the U.S. than at Jerusalem Garden.

48. Stroll Through Nickels Arcade

Just to clear things up right off the bat—Nickels Arcade is not an arcade in the sense that Pinball Pete's is an arcade. Nickels is more of a gorgeous, mini indoor shopping mall. It appears to be just an archway leading to a pretty alley along State Street, but that pretty alley is actually full of shops!

In fact, the pretty skylight-filled alley that is Nickels Arcade has been full of shops for 100 years. In 2017 they celebrated their centennial year, so it totally counts as a historic place in Ann Arbor.

As of the 2017 centennial year, some of the shops inside Nickels Arcade included a gift/collectables store, a coffee shop, and a tobacconist.

49. Catch a Show at The Ark

The Ark: Where Music Lives. It's an apt tagline for a place with live music over 300 nights each year. I always knew it as the most in demand live music venue in the city—lines out the door most nights—but I didn't realize until recently that the Ark is actually world-famous in the live music scene. In others words, it's a big deal.

Their speciality, if you will, is folk music. There are only 400 seats in the whole place, which honestly creates exactly the intimate environment you'd want to listen to amazing folk bands. Tickets aren't cheap, but they aren't exorbitant most of the time; many shows go for $40 a head. The quality of the performances, ticket price, and general prestige would create an elite feel in other places, but not at the Ark. It manages to feel like a chill, casual night out listening to music with friends, just extra memorable.

50. Go Ice Skating at Yost

Ann Arbor is a football town first and foremost, but a hockey town as a close second. The University of Michigan Wolverines hockey team plays at Yost Ice Arena. When it was built in 1923 it was the largest field house in the United States. Between the massive Yost Arena and colossal Big House, it's no wonder Ann Arbor has so many devoted sports fans. And there are always seats for more. You can watch a hockey game here at Yost, or go for a skate yourself! It's one of the coolest places I've ever gone ice skating, just because of the awe-inspiring size. Knowing that you're skating where champions have played makes it even more thrilling.

Top Reasons to Book This Trip

- **Culture**: Ann Arbor has such an individualistic, quirky culture and feel to it. There are as many hippies and free spirits as there are academics and intellectuals. More often than not, people are a mix of both. The whole culture of the town reflects this openminded attitude, from funky restaurants to odd little shops. Though the community is much larger than a small town at this point, everyone still acts like they know everyone else. It's a welcoming place with a community-centered mindset.
- **Food**: I have to admit, I never realized how lucky I was to grow up here. Outside of Chicago I honestly haven't found a city in the Midwest with a more diverse and exciting variety of culinary **options**.
- Events: Ann Arbor has a lot of exciting festivals, concerts, and traditions. It's worth considering planning your trip to coincide with whichever sounds the most fun to you.

Kaisa Wayryn

> TOURIST

GREATER THAN A TOURIST

Visit GreaterThanATourist.com
http://GreaterThanATourist.com

Sign up for the Greater Than a Tourist Newsletter
http://eepurl.com/cxspyf

Follow us on Facebook:
https://www.facebook.com/GreaterThanATourist

Follow us on Pinterest:
http://pinterest.com/GreaterThanATourist

Follow us on Instagram:
http://Instagram.com/GreaterThanATourist

Kaisa Wayryn

> TOURIST

GREATER THAN A TOURIST

Please leave your honest review of this book on Amazon and Goodreads. Thank you.

We appreciate your positive and negative feedback as we try to provide tourist guidance in their next trip from a local.

Our Story

Traveling is a passion of the "Greater than a Tourist" series creator. Lisa studied abroad in college, and for their honeymoon Lisa and her husband toured Europe. During her travels to Malta, an older man tried to give her some advice based on his own experience living on the island since he was a young boy. She was not sure if she should talk to the stranger but was interested in his advice. When traveling to some places she was wary to talk to locals because she was afraid that they weren't being genuine. Through her travels, Lisa learned how much locals had to share with tourists. Lisa created the "Greater Than a Tourist" book series to help connect people with locals. A topic that locals are very passionate about sharing.

Kaisa Wayryn

Notes

Made in the USA
Monee, IL
09 June 2021